Who Is
Jane Goodall?

Who Is Jane Goodall?

by Roberta Edwards

illustrated by John O'Brien

Penguin Workshop

For Pauoa Elementary School in Honolulu, Hawaii—RE
For Terase—JO

PENGUIN WORKSHOP
An Imprint of Penguin Random House LLC, New York

The publisher does not have any control over and does not assume any responsibility for author or third-party websites or their content.

Visit us online at www.penguinrandomhouse.com.

Library of Congress Control Number: 2012019976

ISBN 9780448461922   10 9 8 7 6 5 4 3 2

Part of the *What Is Science & Technology?* Boxed Set, ISBN 9780593090138

Contents

Who Is
Jane Goodall?

When Jane Goodall was a little more than a year old, her father gave her a toy animal. It wasn't a soft and cuddly puppy or kitten or bunny. It was a big chimpanzee!

Why did Jane's father choose a chimp?

It was 1935. A baby chimpanzee had been born at the London Zoo. Jane's parents lived in London and followed the news about the little chimp named Jubilee. Why was it such a big event? Before then, all the zoo's chimps had been born in the wild in Africa.

Jane's toy chimp was named Jubilee, too.

It played music when Jane squeezed its belly. Because Jubilee was so real-looking, some people thought that the chimp was too scary for a baby girl. Jubilee might give little Jane bad dreams. But they were wrong. Jane loved Jubilee and took the toy wherever she went.

As a very young child, Jane Goodall had no idea that she would spend most of her life among chimpanzees—real, live chimpanzees. But that's what she did. The chimps that Jane came to know did not live in a zoo. They roamed free in the forests of eastern Africa.

Over time, the chimps began to treat Jane like just another chimp, a tall, funny-looking, white chimp. Because the chimps accepted her, Jane Goodall was able to learn more about these amazing animals than anybody had before. She saw how chimp mothers cared for their babies. She saw how chimps worked and played together. She learned how chimps showed happiness, fear, anger, and sadness. Most important of all, Jane Goodall proved to the world how alike humans and chimpanzees are.

As for Jubilee the toy chimp, Jane never gave it away. To this day, Jubilee sits on a dresser in the house where Jane lives.

ARE CHIMPANZEES

NO.
MOST LITTLE CHILDREN
WILL LOOK AT A PICTURE OF
A CHIMPANZEE AND SAY IT'S
A MONKEY. BUT CHIMPS ARE
NOT MONKEYS. CHIMPS ARE
APES. SO ARE GORILLAS AND
ORANGUTANS.

APE

MONKEYS?

APES DO NOT HAVE TAILS. ALMOST ALL KINDS OF MONKEYS DO. APES HAVE STRONG ARMS AND CAN SWING FROM TREE BRANCH TO TREE BRANCH. MOST MONKEYS CAN'T DO THIS. THEY RUN ALONG THE TOPS OF BRANCHES. APE SKELETONS LOOK VERY MUCH LIKE HUMAN SKELETONS. MONKEY SKELETONS LOOK MUCH MORE LIKE THE SKELETONS OF DOGS, CATS, AND OTHER SMALL MAMMALS.

MONKEY

MONKEYS, APES, AND HUMANS ALL BELONG TO THE ANIMAL GROUP CALLED PRIMATES. APES ARE OUR CLOSEST RELATIVES IN THE ANIMAL KINGDOM.

Chapter 1
Animal Lover

Jane Goodall was born on April 3, 1934, in London, England. London is one of the world's greatest cities. Jane, however, was far happier in the country. She liked being outdoors, exploring nature. Her family moved outside the city to a house with a yard. What interested her most were animals. All kinds of animals. Learning about them in books was interesting. But facts from books were not enough for Jane.

Jane wanted to find out about animals by watching them herself. One time she dug up some earthworms. She came home and put them under her pillow. Jane wanted to go to sleep with them! Her mother explained that the worms needed to be in their own homes. Little Jane was disappointed, but returned the worms to the garden.

When she was about five, Jane was curious to see how chickens laid eggs. In the backyard at her grandmother's house was a chicken coop.

Here was Jane's chance to watch an egg get laid.

She had Jubilee with her. She crept into the empty chicken coop. Then she waited for a hen

to arrive. Jane stayed so still that the hen didn't notice her. Hour after hour went by. Jane kept waiting and watching. Finally, after five hours, Jane saw what she had hoped for.

Out popped an egg from underneath the chicken!

Jane was excited.

Her family, however, was scared! Her mother had called the police to report that Jane was missing. But when Jane returned to the house, she did not get a scolding. Her mother understood that Jane was not being naughty. She needed to learn about the natural world in her own special way.

Jane's mother was called Vanne. She wrote novels. Jane's father, Mortimer, was an engineer who later became a race car driver. On Jane's fourth birthday, her sister, Judy, was born. Imagine sharing the same birthday as your sister or brother!

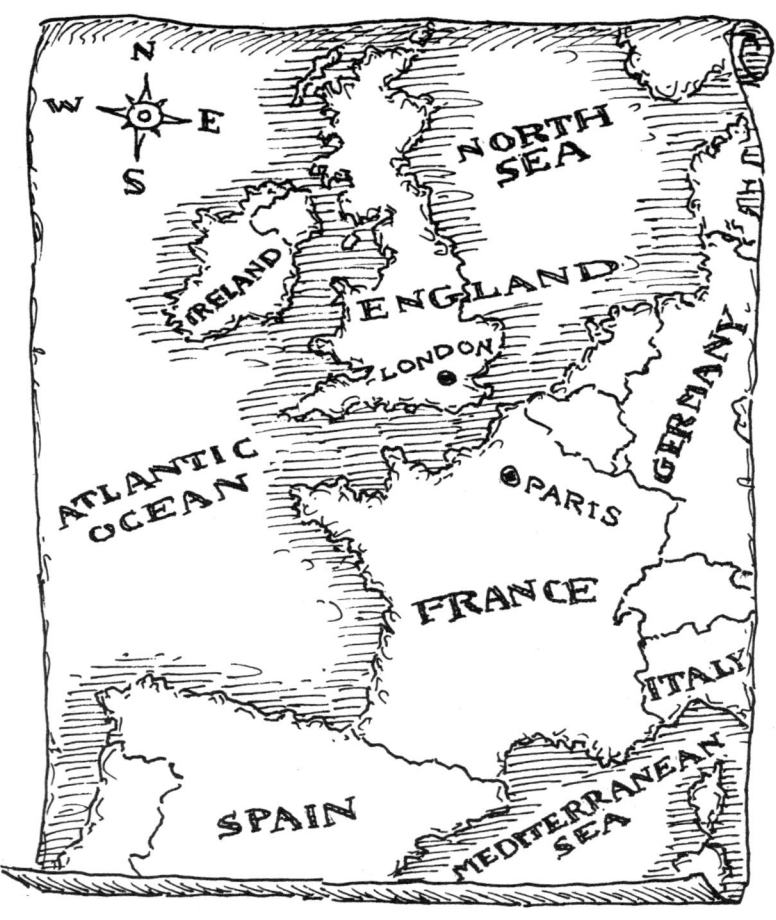

The Goodall girls were young when World
War II broke out in 1939. Adolf Hitler was the
Nazi leader of Germany and Austria. He was trying
to seize control of all of Europe, including England.

Right before the war, Jane's family was living in France. Her father was racing cars there. However, once the war started, the family returned to England. Mortimer joined the British army in the fight against the Nazis. Vanne and her two young daughters moved in with Vanne's mother, who lived in the seaside town of Bournemouth. A little more than one hundred miles from London, Bournemouth was safer than living in London, which the Germans started bombing in September of 1940.

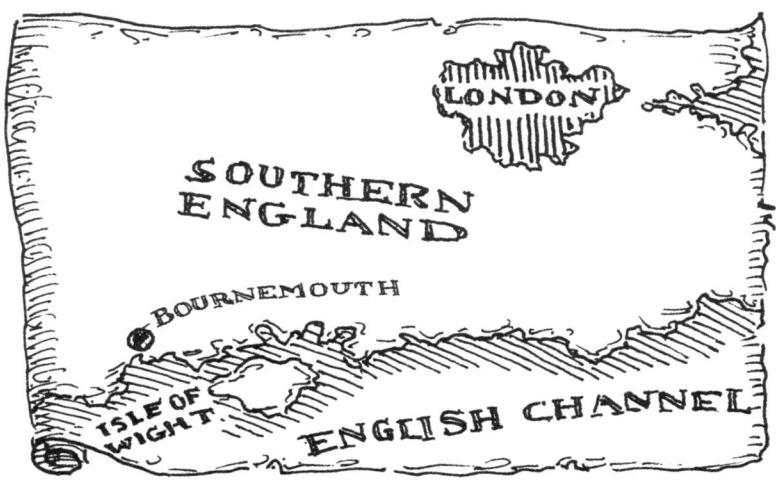

THE BLITZKRIEG

IN GERMAN, BLITZKRIEG MEANS "LIGHTNING WAR." THE TERM IS USED FOR SURPRISE ATTACKS FROM THE AIR. ON SEPTEMBER 7, 1940, GERMAN PLANES FLEW OVER LONDON AND DROPPED BOMBS ON THE CITY. THE ATTACKS LASTED FOR MORE THAN EIGHT MONTHS. IT WAS A FRIGHTENING TIME. OFTEN THE RAIDS HAPPENED AT NIGHT. OFTEN THERE WAS LITTLE OR NO WARNING BEFORE THE BOMBING STARTED. PEOPLE WOULD RUN AND HIDE UNDERGROUND IN SUBWAY STATIONS. WHEN THE BOMBING STOPPED, THEY'D RETURN TO THE STREETS AND SEE RUBBLE WHERE BUILDINGS HAD STOOD ONLY MINUTES BEFORE. ABOUT THIRTY THOUSAND PEOPLE DIED BECAUSE OF THE BOMBINGS. ANOTHER FIFTY THOUSAND WERE INJURED. EVEN SO, THE BRITISH NEVER SURRENDERED TO THE GERMANS. THE WAR ENDED IN EUROPE IN THE SPRING OF 1945 WITH GERMANY'S DEFEAT. THE GOODALLS' FIRST HOME IN LONDON REMAINED STANDING; HOWEVER, MORE THAN ONE MILLION BUILDINGS HAD BEEN DESTROYED. IT TOOK DECADES TO REBUILD LONDON.

In 1943, Vanne and her daughters moved into their own home in Bournemouth. Jane spent the rest of her childhood there. Jane was eight at the time. By then, Mortimer was living apart from his wife and daughters.

Jane was most happy when she was outdoors with a neighborhood dog named Rusty. She started a nature club with her sister and two friends. Jane had lots of rules for the club.

Jane, of course, was the leader. Members had to be able to identify all sorts of different animals. Each member had a code name. The club was fun and interesting. But Jane's friends thought sometimes she was too bossy!

Jane also loved reading books about animals. *The Story of Doctor Dolittle* by Hugh Lofting was one of her favorites. Dr. Dolittle went to Africa and was able to talk to wild animals. Jane understood that she would never be able to carry on a conversation with a tiger or giraffe or monkey. But she knew it was possible to live in Africa close to wild animals. By the time she was ten, she had decided that's exactly what she was going to do with her life.

By 1952, Jane's parents were divorced. She didn't ever lose touch with her father, but she was never close to him the way she was with Vanne.

TARZAN THE JUNGLE HERO

TARZAN, A HUMAN RAISED BY APES IN THE
AFRICAN JUNGLE, WAS THE HERO OF BEST-SELLING
NOVELS BY EDGAR RICE BURROUGHS. THE FIRST
BOOK, *TARZAN OF THE APES*, WAS PUBLISHED IN
1914. THE FIRST TARZAN MOVIE APPEARED IN 1918,
BEFORE THERE WERE "TALKIES." SINCE THEN,
THERE HAVE BEEN ALMOST NINETY MOVIES MADE
ABOUT THE ADVENTURES OF TARZAN. THE MOST
POPULAR ONES CAME OUT IN THE 1930S AND
1940S. THEY STARRED JOHNNY WEISSMULLER,
A FORMER OLYMPIC SWIMMER. TARZAN'S BEST
FRIEND WAS A CHIMP NAMED CHEETAH, AND HIS
GIRLFRIEND WAS NAMED JANE.

JANE GOODALL HAS SAID THAT THE TARZAN
MOVIES MADE A BIG IMPRESSION ON HER.
TARZAN WAS LIVING HER DREAM LIFE!

Jane was graduating from high school. Although she had been a very good student, there was not enough money for college. So Jane moved to London and took a job as a secretary. The city was a thrilling place to live. However, Jane told her mother and grandmother that her work was dull. It made her "miserable." Through a friend, she found a job at a company that made documentary films. That was much more interesting.

Still, Jane never stopped dreaming of Africa—to live there and find work studying animals in their natural homes.

The odds were not in Jane's favor. First of all, in the 1950s, scientists studied animals in zoos or labs, not in the wild. Animal scientists had years of education; Jane Goodall had no college degree. And at the time, even women with degrees were limited in their career choices. Most became teachers or went into nursing.

So how would Jane find a way to live the life she longed for?

Chapter 2
An Invitation

In 1956, a letter came that changed Jane Goodall's life. It was from an old school friend named Clo. Clo's family had bought a farm in Kenya, Africa. Clo wanted Jane to visit. Did Jane think twice about going?

Of course not!

Traveling to Africa was expensive. Living in London was expensive, too. So Jane moved back home with her mother in Bournemouth. She saved up money for the trip by working as a waitress. Jane was a very good waitress. She could carry as many as thirteen plates balanced on her arms!

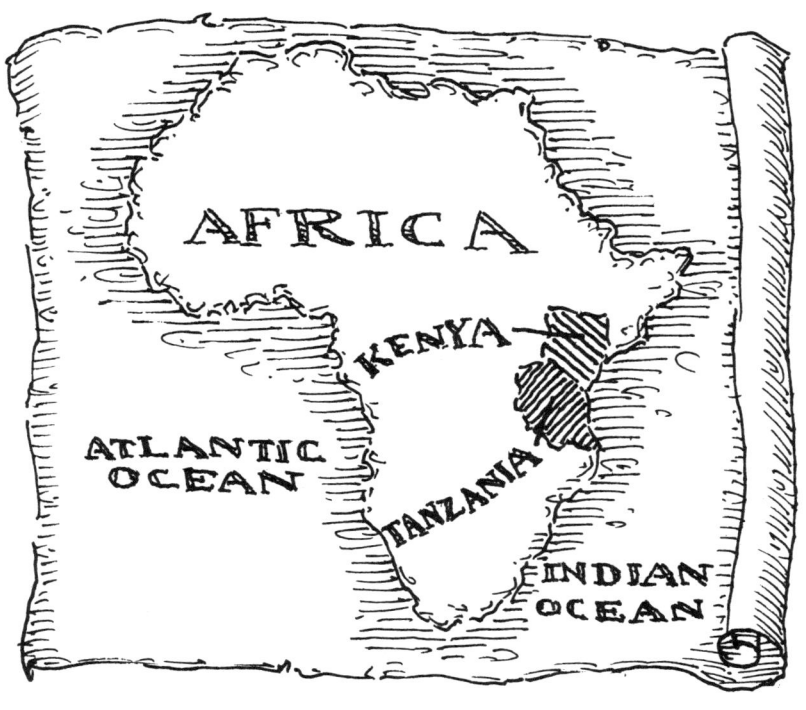

On March 13, 1957, Jane's African adventure
began. She was turning twenty-three. In England,
she boarded a ship that arrived in Kenya three
weeks later. From the city of Mombasa, she took a
train inland. It was April 3—her birthday! After a
long drive on dirt roads, Jane reached the farm in
time for dinner and birthday cake.

That very first day, Jane saw a giraffe. It wasn't in a cage. It was running by the side of a road. She could hardly believe it! What a terrific birthday present that was!

Jane knew that she couldn't stay at the farm for more than a few weeks. She was a guest, after all. She didn't want to overstay her welcome. What she needed was a job that would keep her in Africa.

Jane was in luck. At a party, she met someone who arranged a meeting between Jane and the famous scientist Louis Leakey. He and his wife Mary were British citizens. But Kenya was their home.

LOUIS AND MARY LEAKEY

LOUIS LEAKEY

LOUIS LEAKEY WAS BORN IN AUGUST 1903 IN KENYA. HIS PARENTS HAD BEEN BORN IN GREAT BRITAIN. THEY WENT TO AFRICA TO TEACH THE CHRISTIAN RELIGION TO THE KIKUYU TRIBE. LOUIS'S VERY FIRST HOME WAS A TINY HUT WITH A DIRT FLOOR. THE ROOF WAS MADE OF THATCH AND LEAKED. GROWING UP, HE FELT MUCH MORE AFRICAN THAN BRITISH. HIS FRIENDS WERE ALL AFRICANS, AND WHEN HE WAS A TEENAGER, THE KIKUYU PEOPLE HONORED HIM WITH MEMBERSHIP IN THEIR TRIBE.

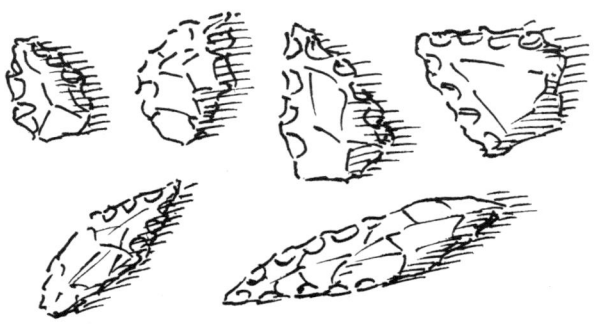

AT THIRTEEN, LOUIS FOUND SOME STONE TOOLS MADE BY EARLY HUMANS. THIS DISCOVERY SPARKED A LIFELONG CAREER STUDYING THE ORIGINS OF HUMAN BEINGS. ALONG WITH HIS SECOND WIFE, MARY LEAKEY, HE HUNTED FOR FOSSILS OF HUMAN ANCESTORS. THE LEAKEYS WORKED IN AN AREA

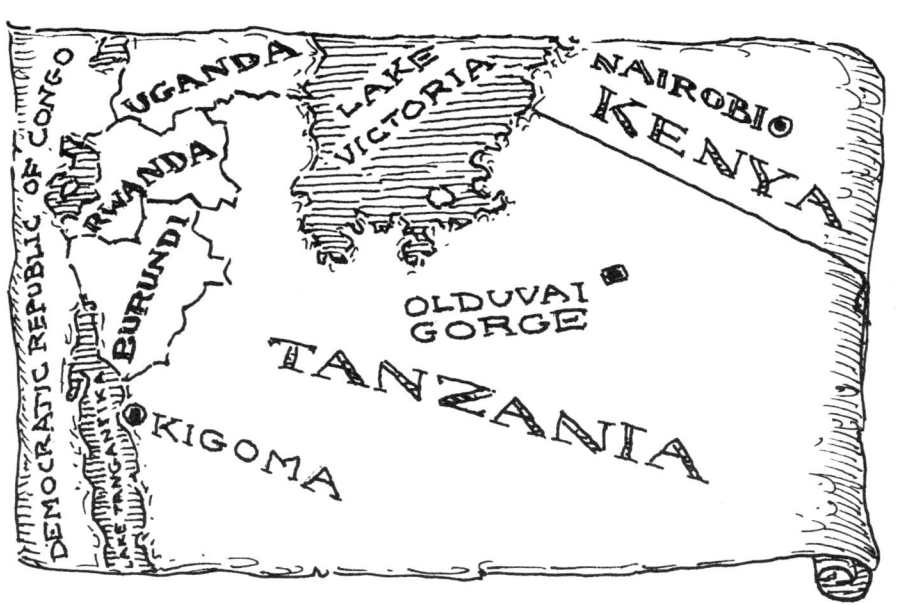

CALLED OLDUVAI GORGE IN TANZANIA. (AT THE TIME, THE COUNTRY WAS CALLED TANGANYIKA.)

BESIDES BEING A FAMOUS FOSSIL HUNTER, LOUIS LEAKEY WORKED HARD TO PROTECT THE WILDLIFE OF AFRICA. HE ALSO HELPED THE CAREERS OF TWO YOUNG WOMEN WHO WANTED TO STUDY WILD ANIMALS IN AFRICA. ONE WAS JANE GOODALL. THE OTHER WAS DIAN FOSSEY, WHO BECAME FAMOUS FOR HER WORK WITH GORILLAS. *GORILLAS IN THE MIST* IS A MOVIE ABOUT DIAN FOSSEY AND HER WORK.

LOUIS LEAKEY DIED IN 1972 WHILE VISITING JANE GOODALL'S MOTHER, VANNE, IN ENGLAND.

At Olduvai Gorge in the plains of east Africa, the Leakeys led groups on digs to find fossils. Not dinosaur fossils. The Leakeys were looking for fossils of the very earliest humans. Most scientists at the time thought that the first humans were from Asia. Louis believed they were from Africa. And he was right!

In 1960, he came upon fossils of a very early human species. It came to be known as *Homo habilis*. *Homo habilis* lived on Earth from about 2.3 to 1.4 million years ago. It looked more like an ape than like a modern human being. It had a small head, was short, and had very long arms.

HOMO HABILIS

From the moment Louis Leakey met Jane, he liked her. She had a shy manner. But he could tell she was smart and had a spirit of adventure. He offered her a job. Naturally, Jane took it!

Jane worked as Leakey's secretary at a museum in the city of Nairobi, Kenya. But right away, Leakey gave her the chance to dig for fossils at Olduvai Gorge.

Jane had never done this type of work before.
She didn't know anything about digging for fossils.
But she was a fast learner. For hours every day,
Jane picked away at the clay and rocks with small
tools. Sometimes she unearthed a bone of a
creature from the distant past. But usually she
found nothing. The work was tiring. During
the dry season, the Olduvai
Gorge was like a desert.

Even so, it was a wonderful
time for Jane. She wrote that
"it was wild, untouched Africa.
There were all the animals of my
childhood dreams." She saw
lions, a rhinoceros, and loads
of gazelles. She saw dik-diks,

RHINOCEROS

GAZELLES

DIK-DIKS

which are little
antelopes, the size of a fox terrier.
From Louis Leakey, Jane
learned about the chimpanzees

living in the forests near Lake Tanganyika. They were long-haired chimpanzees. Leakey was interested in chimps because he believed that they had much in common with early humans.

Wild chimps are found only in Africa, nowhere else in the world. One study had been done on wild chimps. However, it had lasted for less than three months. Leakey thought that much more time was needed to learn anything important about the chimps. Jane had no experience. This was her first time in Africa. Yet he believed Jane Goodall was the right person for the job.

Jane did, too!

In July 1960, she moved to the Gombe Stream Game Reserve in what is now the country of Tanzania. First she met the two African scouts who protected the area. Then Jane set off to take a quick look around.

Her life's work was about to begin.

Chapter 3
Life in the Wild

What was it like to live at Gombe Stream in 1960?

Steel-gray mountains rose up from the eastern shore of Lake Tanganyika. In the valleys between the slopes were forests. It was completely wild. There were no tourists, no safari groups with cameras, and no fancy lodges to stay in. Jane lived near the lake in a little clearing by a small stream. She was cut

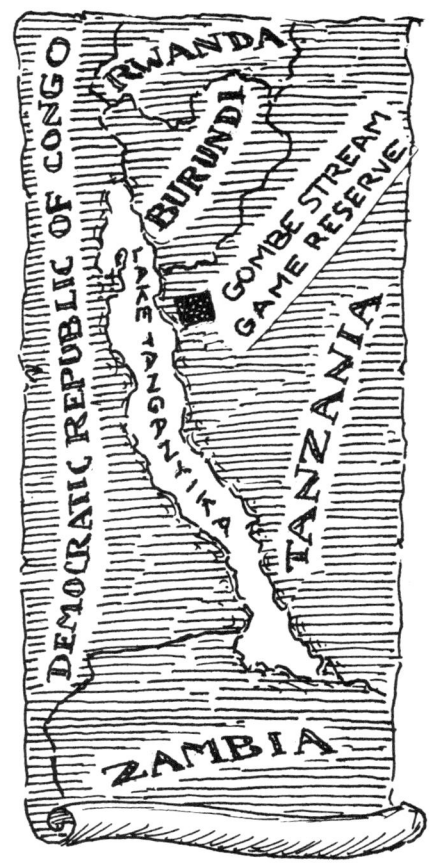

off from the rest of the world. Even the town of Kigoma was an hour boat ride away.

Who besides Jane lived at the campsite? In addition to a cook named Dominic, there was one very important person.

Jane's mother, Vanne.

Vanne stayed with Jane for the first four months at Gombe. Mother and daughter lived in the same old army tent together. It had two cots and a separate area for washing up. Mosquito netting covered the front of the tent. Their toilet was outside. It was a deep hole surrounded by a fence.

Vanne was a middle-aged woman. Living like this was hard for Jane; it had to be twice as hard for Vanne. Yet officials in Africa had refused to let Jane go off alone to Gombe. They were worried about the safety of a young woman living alone.

There was no way Vanne was going to let Jane pass up this chance to live with the chimps.

Already past fifty, Vanne packed up for Africa. It is easy to see where Jane's bravery came from!

Having Vanne share those first months meant so much to Jane. It was better than having a best friend along! In the evening when she returned to camp, Vanne was there. They'd have dinner and chat. Vanne kept Jane company while she wrote up her notes from that day. At first she wrote by hand on lined paper. Later she got a portable typewriter.

What did Vanne do all day while Jane was out exploring?

Vanne set up a little clinic. She provided basic health care to the local families. She handed out aspirin and cleaned cuts. Sometimes she helped deliver babies!

About once every two weeks, Jane and Vanne went by boat into Kigoma. In town, they picked up mail and enough food and supplies to last until the next trip. They'd stock up on eggs, baked beans, and sausages. At the fruit and vegetable market, they bought bananas, green and yellow oranges, and passion fruit.

Two African scouts lived in huts not far from Jane's camp. One always made the trip into Kigoma with Jane and Vanne. It was not considered proper for two white women to travel alone!

The main job of the scouts was to help Jane find her way through the forests. These forests were home to the chimpanzees. Jane, however, did not like having a scout along.

Why?

Two people made more noise than one person alone in the forest. And noises scared away the chimps. Also, the scouts didn't like to start off as

early as Jane. She was always up before dawn! And
often the scouts wanted to head back to camp way
before Jane did. So after a while, the scouts let
Jane explore by herself. Now she was free to go at

her own pace. Sometimes she sat on the ground.
Sometimes she perched in trees. She could stay
overnight if she wanted. Plus, being alone made
it easier to remain unseen by the chimps.

Because of how far away the chimps were,
Jane carried binoculars with her. She took a

tin box with her, too. It contained a sweater,
a blanket, some food, coffee, and a mug. Jane
always wore her hair in a ponytail. And she wore
the same outfit every day—a tan shirt and tan
shorts. Colorful clothes would make her stand
out too much. She wanted to blend in with the

background. Often she had to crawl through
tangled vines. She got bitten by flies and scratched
by sharp grass. But nothing stopped her.

Was Jane Goodall afraid of anything?

Yes. She was
scared of leopards.
She knew the
smell of leopards,
and many times
Jane caught their
scent in the forest.
One time she had
to climb a tree
to get away from
a leopard. She
was lucky: The
leopard did not
climb up after
her. Instead, the
leopard pooped
on the rock where
Jane had been
sitting only a few
minutes before!

Jane couldn't always see chimps, so how did she know where to look?

She knew the sounds that chimps make. Hearing certain cries tipped her off that chimps were in the area. Jane would pick out a spot and sit. She'd stay for hours, quietly waiting and watching. Some days she didn't see any chimps. Even so, she was sure they were watching her. Other days, she saw many. Sometimes a few large males would gather together. Sometimes she spotted a mother with her young. Sometimes she caught sight of bigger groups of males, females, and young chimps.

The trouble was that the chimps were always so far off. And they never were doing anything very interesting. Jane hoped to spy on chimps playing together. Or watch a mother caring for a baby chimp. Instead, all she saw were chimps searching

for food. They'd climb up fig trees and pull off fruit. However, the minute Jane tried to move closer to them, the chimps would run away.

How was she going to learn anything that mattered?

Chapter 4
The Chimps

Jane was discouraged by how little progress
she was making with the chimps. Then, to make
matters worse, she and Vanne both got sick. Very
sick. Most likely both women had come down
with malaria. They had no drugs with them to
treat the disease. Jane had been told that there was
no malaria at Gombe, so she didn't take medicine
along. Jane blamed herself for that!

For two weeks, Jane and her mother never left
their tent. All they did was lie in bed and sweat.

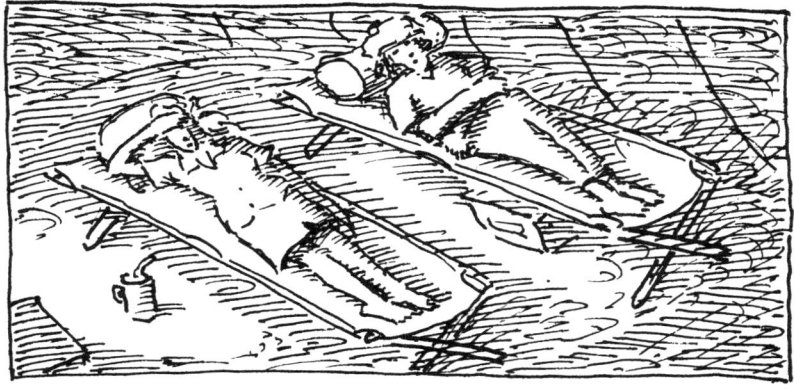

MALARIA

FEMALE MOSQUITO

MALARIA IS ONE OF THE MOST WIDESPREAD DISEASES IN THE WORLD. PEOPLE CATCH IT FROM BEING BITTEN BY A CERTAIN KIND OF MOSQUITO. MALARIA DOES DAMAGE TO THE LIVER AND TO BLOOD CELLS. THE SYMPTOMS ARE HIGH FEVERS, VOMITING, CHILLS, AND BAD HEADACHES.

PEOPLE IN AFRICA SOUTH OF THE SAHARA DESERT ARE MOST AT RISK FOR MALARIA. INSECT SPRAYS CAN KILL INDOOR MOSQUITOES. DRUGS CAN TREAT THE DISEASE. BUT AS OF YET THERE IS NO VACCINE TO PREVENT MALARIA. MORE THAN ONE MILLION PEOPLE STILL DIE OF IT EVERY YEAR.

For many days, Vanne's fever rose as high as 105 degrees.

Both Jane and Vanne were lucky; they recovered. The minute she felt well enough, Jane returned to the forests.

At last, her patience paid off. It was October. Vanne had gone home to England. Jane was on her own. She began exploring an area she called the Peak. Every day, rain or shine, she climbed up the steep slope of the Peak into the forest.

Little by little, the chimps became used to Jane watching them. One day she saw a female hold out her hand to a male, who kissed it! She saw two baby chimps play tug-of-war with a twig.

Jane could tell many of the chimps apart, and she gave them names.

Flo was an old female chimp. Jane liked Flo a lot. She was a very popular chimp, although—to Jane, at least—Flo was funny-looking. She had a big round nose and torn ears. Flo had a baby. Jane called her Fifi. And she called Fifi's older brothers Faben and Figan. Flo was a caring mother. She protected Fifi from the rain. She carefully

FLO   FIGAN

groomed her young. (Grooming means cleaning their fur.) Flo was a playful mother, but she was also firm. She never let her children get out of line!

Olly was Flo's friend. Olly was also a female. Her face was very long, and her lips jiggled a lot. Another chimp—a male—looked a lot like Olly. Jane was quite sure he was Olly's brother. She named him William.

In animal studies, animals are usually given

FIFI   FABEN

numbers, not names. In fact, many scientists think it's a bad idea to name animals that are being studied. They worry that it will make the animals seem too human.

Jane definitely did not think of the chimps as humans. But she did see the chimps as individuals. They had different personalities. William was timid and fearful. Gilka was a show-off, always looking for attention. Frodo was a bully, a dangerous bully.

One time Jane had been watching Frodo when suddenly he charged. He beat and kicked her.

Frodo started to leave, then came back, beat Jane more, and dragged her to the edge of a cliff. What did Frodo do next?

He threw her over the side. It was a steep drop, but luckily there were bushes that stopped Jane's fall. Even so, she was banged up pretty bad.

CAN CHIMPS LEARN

FOR MANY YEARS, SCIENTISTS TRIED TO TEACH CHIMPS TO MAKE THE SAME SOUNDS AS HUMANS DO. NO ONE EVER HAD SUCCESS. CHIMPS' VOCAL CORDS MAKE IT IMPOSSIBLE FOR THEM TO SPEAK.

THEN, IN 1966, TWO RESEARCHERS TRIED SOMETHING DIFFERENT. THEY BEGAN TEACHING AMERICAN SIGN LANGUAGE TO A TEN-MONTH-OLD CHIMP NAMED WASHOE. IN TIME, WASHOE LEARNED TO MAKE THE SIGNS FOR ABOUT 130 WORDS.

SIGN FOR WATER + SIGN FOR BIRD =

HUMAN LANGUAGE?

ACCORDING TO HER TEACHERS, WASHOE COULD ALSO "CREATE" A WORD WHEN SHE DIDN'T KNOW THE SIGN FOR SOMETHING. ON SEEING A SWAN, WASHOE MADE THE SIGNS FOR BOTH *WATER* AND *BIRD*. DID THIS MEAN WASHOE UNDERSTOOD WORDS? IT CERTAINLY SEEMED SO. HOWEVER, TO MANY SCIENTISTS, THIS DID NOT COUNT AS TRULY LEARNING A LANGUAGE. LANGUAGE INVOLVES MAKING SENTENCES, USING GRAMMAR, AND HAVING CONVERSATIONS. NONE OF THE CHIMPS COULD DO ANYTHING LIKE THIS.

SWAN

In many ways, the chimps behaved like humans. Though unable to speak, they had their own means of communicating. Jane learned to tell what their different grunts, pants, and screams meant. For example, chimps greeted one another with soft panting grunts. A certain loud scream was a cry for help.

Chimps, like humans, expressed feelings through gestures. They hugged and kissed one another. They bowed to show respect.

They patted friends on the back for comfort. They also shook their fists or threw rocks to show anger. To Jane, naming the chimps just felt right.

Did Jane have a favorite chimp?

Yes!

Jane called him David Graybeard because of the silvery hair around his chin. In one of her

DAVID GRAYBEARD

books, she wrote, "David Graybeard had the most beautiful eyes of them all, large and lustrous, set wide apart. They somehow expressed his whole personality."

David Graybeard had a calm nature and was not afraid of Jane. He was the first chimp who seemed to accept her. One day, Jane held out a piece of fruit to David Graybeard. He came up to her, took the fruit, and then held her hand in his.

What a special moment that was for Jane!

David Graybeard taught Jane Goodall a lot
about chimpanzees.

For a long time, scientists believed that chimpanzees were herbivores. Herbivores are animals that eat only fruits and vegetables. They do not eat meat.

But one day, Jane saw David Graybeard and several other chimpanzees in the upper branches of a tree. They were grouped around something. The something turned out to be a dead piglet.

David Graybeard handed out pieces of meat to the others; he also let them bite off meat themselves. For three hours, the chimps fed on the piglet. What Jane watched proved that chimps are omnivores. They eat meat as well as lots of food from plants.

This was interesting news. But a couple of weeks later, Jane came upon David Graybeard doing something even more amazing.

It was a day of heavy rains. Jane was tired and dripping wet. Through her binoculars, she spotted David Graybeard. He was squatting down by a nest of termites. Termites are insects that chimps like to eat. Termite nests are like big mounds with a hole at the top. David Graybeard was poking a long blade of grass into the hole of the nest to fish out termites. David was using the blade of grass as a tool. It did a great job of supplying David Graybeard with tasty termites.

Why was this so amazing?

Up until 1960, scientists believed that humans were the only animals able to make tools. Making tools may not sound like such a big deal, but think about it.

A dog digs a hole with its front paws. It does not know how to make a shovel to dig a deeper hole more easily. Also, its paws are not able to hold a shovel.

An animal needs a big, smart brain to make tools. An animal also needs hands with thumbs in order to grasp tools.

Chimps have big brains. They also have thumbs. Still, scientists did not think that chimps knew how to make tools. But Jane watched David Graybeard do exactly that.

DOG'S PAW   CHIMPANZEE'S HAND

Once David Graybeard was gone, Jane went over to get a closer look at the grass tools. Jane tried pushing one into the nest herself. Sure enough, she could feel termites grab hold of the grass. When she took out the blade of grass, the termites were there kicking their legs about.

In her book *Reason for Hope*, Jane wrote that "it was hard for me to believe what I had seen. It had long been thought that we were the only creatures on earth that used and made tools." What she saw proved that was not so.

Another time, Jane came upon David Graybeard and a big, strong chimp named Goliath. They were fishing for termites together. They kept a supply of extra grass tools in case any broke. Sometimes they picked up twigs and stripped off any leaves before using them. Again, this may not sound astounding at first. But the chimps were making changes to the twigs so that they worked better as tools. Chimps also used chewed clumps of leaves as sponges to soak up drinking water. And whole leaves made good washcloths for cleaning themselves.

Louis Leakey was thrilled when Jane sent news of David Graybeard's "fishing" trips. Leakey knew he'd been right about sending Jane Goodall to Gombe! He spread the word of what she was learning. It did not take long for the National Geographic Society to give Jane enough money to stay at Gombe for another year.

It was the best gift in the world.

HOW ALIKE ARE
CHIMPS AND HUMANS?

IT MAY SURPRISE YOU TO KNOW THIS, BUT A HUMAN BEING IS MORE LIKE A CHIMP THAN A MOUSE IS LIKE A RAT!

WHY ARE HUMANS AND CHIMPS SO ALIKE? THE REASON IS THAT THEY COME FROM A COMMON ANCESTOR— AN APELIKE CREATURE WHO

HUMAN   CHIMPANZEE

LIVED ON EARTH SOMEWHERE BETWEEN FOUR AND EIGHT MILLION YEARS AGO. EVEN A QUICK LOOK AT HUMANS AND CHIMPS SHOWS MANY

SIMILARITIES. HUMAN AND CHIMP FACES ARE ALIKE. THEY SHOW THE EMOTIONS THEY FEEL, LIKE HAPPINESS, SADNESS, AND FEAR. BOTH HUMANS AND CHIMPS HAVE HANDS WITH THUMBS.

WHAT CAN'T BE SEEN IS THE BRAIN INSIDE THE SKULL OF A CHIMP OR HUMAN. BOTH HAVE A LARGE BRAIN FOR THEIR BODY SIZE. THAT'S WHAT MAKES THEM SMART ANIMALS.

THE DNA OF HUMANS AND CHIMPS IS ALMOST EXACTLY THE SAME. DNA DETERMINES THE MAKEUP OF ANY ANIMAL. THERE'S JUST A LITTLE MORE THAN 1 PERCENT DIFFERENCE BETWEEN THE TWO SPECIES. YET THAT LITTLE DIFFERENCE COUNTS FOR A LOT. IT ACCOUNTS FOR WHY CHIMPS DON'T UNDERSTAND HOW TO GROW FOOD AND WHY THEY ARE UNABLE TO SPEAK OR MAKE ART OR MUSIC. AND ALTHOUGH CHIMPS DO MAKE SIMPLE TOOLS, THEY CAN'T MAKE MACHINES OR THINK THE SAME KIND OF HARD, DEEP THOUGHTS AS HUMANS.

AND HERE IS AN ODD FACT: UNLIKE HUMANS, CHIMPS DO NOT CRY TEARS.

Chapter 5
Hugo Arrives

National Geographic magazine wanted the world to know about Jane Goodall and the chimps of Gombe. The magazine hoped to publish an article as soon as possible—an article with photographs. In August 1963, Jane's first article appeared in the magazine. It was called "My Life Among Wild Chimpanzees."

Jane could not take the photographs for the magazine herself. It was hard enough following the chimps around with binoculars and taking notes. But she also was not eager for a photographer to come join her.

Why?

She was afraid that it would disrupt her work. The chimps were finally allowing her in their midst. She was able to get much closer to them— they were sometimes only yards away. In time, David Graybeard began coming to the camp to visit. He'd take handfuls of bananas from Jane. Soon, other chimps came, too. If a stranger suddenly appeared on the scene, the chimps were sure to be fearful and hide from Jane again. All the trust she had built would be destroyed.

Jane's suggestion was for her sister, Judy, to join her in Gombe. Judy would take photos. Jane and Judy looked a lot alike. Jane figured that the chimps might accept her sister.

Having Judy's company was very welcome. The two sisters would go off together into the forests.

Jane continued watching the chimps while Judy took photos. The trouble was, Judy's photos weren't good enough for magazines.

Once again, Louis Leakey found a way to help Jane. He arranged for a young photographer who worked for *National Geographic* to go to Gombe. His name was Hugo van Lawick. Hugo was interested in everything about the chimps. And Jane was wrong about how the chimps would react to Hugo. They didn't mind having him around. He was able to catch chimps patrolling their home

range. He took pictures of two chimps in a
fight to become the group leader. His photos
were wonderful. In 1963, *National Geographic*

magazine ran an article about Jane and the
chimps. It was the first of many.

Louis Leakey was very happy that such a

famous magazine recognized the importance of Jane's work. However, Louis also wanted the scientific world to accept Jane as an expert on chimpanzees. The fact that Jane didn't have a college degree worked against her. So Louis Leakey helped to get Jane admitted to Cambridge University in England.

CAMBRIDGE UNIVERSITY

Cambridge is one of the finest universities in the world. Even though she had never gone to college, Jane was allowed to study for an advanced degree. Cambridge decided that her work with the chimps counted as a college degree. Of course, studying at Cambridge meant being gone for part of the year from Africa. Every day away was hard for Jane. But by 1965, Jane completed all the work for her doctorate. She was now Dr. Jane Goodall.

HUGO VAN LAWICK

HUGO VAN LAWICK WAS BORN IN INDONESIA ON APRIL 10, 1937. HIS FAMILY WERE DUTCH ARISTOCRATS. HUGO WAS A BARON!

LIKE JANE, HUGO WAS FASCINATED BY THE ANIMAL WORLD FROM THE TIME HE WAS A CHILD. HE, TOO, WANTED TO LIVE AMONG WILD CREATURES IN ORDER TO LEARN ABOUT THEM. JANE TOOK NOTES ON EVERYTHING SHE SAW. HUGO, HOWEVER, RECORDED EVERYTHING THROUGH PHOTOGRAPHS AND FILM. IN 1959, HE TRAVELED TO KENYA TO WORK FOR A DUTCH FILM COMPANY. BY 1962, HE WAS COVERING EASTERN AFRICA FOR THE NATIONAL GEOGRAPHIC SOCIETY. THE SOCIETY'S

MAGAZINE SENT HIM TO GOMBE. HE WAS TO PHOTOGRAPH THE GROUP OF CHIMPS THAT JANE GOODALL WAS STUDYING.

HUGO STAYED ON IN TANZANIA, CONTINUING HIS LIFE'S WORK. BESIDES CHIMPANZEES, HE BECAME INTERESTED IN OTHER CREATURES OF THE AREA—GOLDEN JACKALS, HYENAS, AND LEOPARDS. HE WON MANY PRIZES, INCLUDING EIGHT EMMYS FOR TELEVISION SHOWS.

HUGO VAN LAWICK LIVED IN AFRICA FOR MORE THAN FORTY YEARS. THIRTY OF THEM HE SPENT LIVING IN A TENT. HE DIED IN 2002 AND WAS BURIED IN TANZANIA, THE LAND HE LOVED SO MUCH.

Chapter 6
Fame

Right away, Jane and Hugo van Lawick became close friends. They had very different personalities. Hugo was a stiffer, more formal person than Jane was. However, they worked very well alongside each other. They were a team. Each night they talked excitedly about what they had seen the chimps doing. In time, Hugo and Jane fell in love. In London, on March 28, 1964, they were married. On top of the wedding cake was a little clay model of David Graybeard. On the walls hung pictures of David and Goliath, Flo and her daughter Fifi, and many of Jane and Hugo's other chimp "friends."

The National Geographic Society provided more money for Jane's work. Over time, the camp grew. Many young graduate students went to join Jane at Gombe. In 1965, buildings were erected, then covered with grass to blend in with the forest.

More and more information was gathered about the chimp community. For instance, before Gombe, scientists had thought that a chimpanzee group was made up of one male and lots of females.

That's not so.

A group is made up of many males and females. There were around fifty in the group that Jane knew. The group lives within a home range. An adult male is always the leader and may stay in charge for as long as ten years. When the leader becomes too old and weak, most often younger males will fight one another to be the next leader.

Goliath was the leader, or alpha male, when Jane first went to Gombe. Later, a chimp named Mike replaced Goliath. Mike was not a big, strong chimp. But he was clever. He acted big and strong, which made the other males fear and respect him.

Among the females, Flo was the most respected. In 1964, she had another baby. Jane and Hugo called him Flint. They did not know who Flint's father was. Male and female chimps do not pair off and live together. Nor does a male chimp take part in raising his young. The mother chimp cares for the young by herself.

Flo often came into the camp with her new baby. So Jane saw close-up how an infant chimp develops.

Like a newborn human baby, a newborn chimp is helpless. Flint depended on Flo for milk, to keep him safe, and to carry him around. For the first five or six months, Flint clung to the fur on his mother's belly. Afterward, Flo made him ride on her back. By the time most chimps are a year old, they can walk steadily. But chimps will ride on their mothers until they are about two years old. After that they travel on their own, still staying close to their mother.

Flint had two much older brothers, Figan and Faben. His sister Fifi was four when he was born. Fifi was fascinated with little Flint. She wanted to be around him all the time. When he was older, Fifi would hold him and take him for rides on her back. She was learning to be a mother!

Flo was an excellent mother. In fact, most of the female chimps at Gombe were good mothers. They kept their babies very close to them.

The chimp mothers gave their babies lots of
love and attention. They cuddled them. They
protected them. They did not punish their babies
for misbehaving. Instead, a chimp mother would
distract a baby to stop naughty behavior. They
let their babies have lots of playtime. The little
chimps chased and tickled one another and played
games like tug-of-war.

Jane believed that watching the chimps taught her a lot about good mothering. In 1967, she and Hugo had a son. His first name was also Hugo, but everyone called him Grub.

There was an important question of safety now that Jane had a child. A baby would not know to be careful around chimps. And chimps had been known to attack human infants. So Jane and Hugo moved to a house by the lake to keep Grub safe. Jane spent most of her time caring for him while students went into the forests to observe the chimps.

Little Grub loved to swim in the lake and go fishing.

Did he come to love the chimps as much as his parents did?

No!

When Grub was quite young, a chimp bit his finger. Grub had been trying to give it some food. After that, Grub kept his distance from the animals.

Meanwhile, Jane and Hugo continued working as partners. They wrote books together and made many films together. Jane wrote many books by herself that became very popular. One book, *In the Shadow of Man*, first came out in 1971. It became a best seller and has been translated into about fifty languages.

In December 1965, an hour-long program appeared on national TV in the United States. It was called *Miss Goodall and the Wild Chimpanzees*. Viewers were fascinated by the chimps. They were equally fascinated by the pretty, young Jane Goodall. Jane became famous. Over the

years, Jane became *world* famous. Perhaps it was
difficult for Hugo to be married to a superstar.
Though they remained friends, after ten years of
marriage, Hugo and Jane got divorced.

DEREK BRYCESON

Jane remarried in 1975. Her second husband was named Derek Bryceson. He worked in the government of Tanzania and lived in the city of Dar es Salaam much of the time. Although the couple was often apart, many of Jane's friends considered Derek the love of her life. He died in 1980 of cancer.

Chapter 7
The Dark Years

In zoos, chimps can live to be sixty-five years old. In the wild, they don't live nearly as long—perhaps forty or fifty years.

Why?

It is much harder to survive in the wild. Babies have the hardest time of all. Baboons may attack and kill them. Some years, there isn't enough food to go around. Chimps in the wild also catch diseases such as pneumonia or the flu, which zoo chimps are protected from.

BABOONS

In 1966, an outbreak of polio swept through the forest at Gombe. It killed several chimps and left others with crippled arms. (Polio is a disease that can also strike humans, but since the 1950s there has been a vaccine to prevent it.)

Flo managed to avoid polio. But in August 1972, old age caught up with her. Jane wrote a letter to her family that Flo had died. In it, she said, "I had known her for eleven years and I had loved her." Jane also wrote about Flo in London's *Sunday Times* newspaper. It was the first time that there had been an obituary for an animal. Flo was probably around fifty years old when she died. Her youngest, Flint, was eight and a half years old by then. He was strong and well past childhood. But he could not bear life without Flo. Three days after her death, Jane saw him staring at Flo's empty nest.

Flint stopped eating. He stopped traveling with the group. Instead, he stayed by the spot where Flo had died. He soon fell ill. There was nothing Jane or the students could do to help Flint. His death on September 15 was heartbreaking.

In 2012, on the television show *60 Minutes*, Jane said that at first she had thought chimps were like humans, "only nicer." Perhaps she had Flo and David Graybeard in mind when she said that. However, the longer Jane remained among the chimps, the more she saw that some of her early ideas about them were wrong. Chimps had a very dark and violent side, just like humans.

In 1974, a war broke out, a war within the chimp community. A couple of years earlier, the chimps at Gombe had split into two groups. Both groups remained in the home range. But they stayed in different parts of it.

The war started after six male chimps from one group attacked a male chimp from the other group. The chimp was beaten savagely and left to die. The attacks went on for almost three years, until one group was nearly wiped out. Jane wrote about the battles in the May 1979 issue of *National Geographic* magazine.

And then there was Passion.

Jane had observed Passion for years. Passion seemed to not have an ounce of kindness. She neglected her daughter, Pom. It was pitiful watching little Pom beg for her mother's attention.

Uncaring was one thing. But in 1974, Passion did something so awful, the researchers at Gombe were stunned.

Jane was away from camp, but heard the story upon her return.

Gilka had just given birth to an infant daughter. Like Flo, Gilka was a loving mother. She was sitting in the sun, cradling her tiny newborn, when all of a sudden Passion appeared. Without warning, she charged at Gilka. Gilka tried to escape, but polio had crippled her hand. She could not run fast enough. Passion snatched Gilka's baby, and after killing it, fed on it until

every last bit was gone.

There had been several instances of babies suddenly disappearing. Now Jane believed that Passion had probably killed them, too. Why did she behave this way? Jane had no answer. But Passion's actions forced Jane to change her thinking about chimps.

Another awful event struck the camp the following year, in May 1975. This time the chimps were not involved.

Armed with grenades and guns, a group of men came into Gombe and kidnapped four students. They demanded money for their freedom. A ransom was paid, and the students all returned unharmed. But after that, no more foreign students lived at Gombe. Instead, trained field staff from Tanzania did the work of American and European research students.

Grub was growing up. Now he spent the school year in England. It was lonely without him. Jane spent less and less time at Gombe. The nature of her work was changing. In 1977, the Jane Goodall

Institute was founded. Its goal is to continue the study of chimps at Gombe and protect them, as well as other wild animals.

Then, in 1986, Jane attended a conference with other scientists who studied chimps. They discussed an alarming issue. Unless steps were taken, wild chimps might become extinct. One day there simply would be no more of these amazing creatures left.

Why?

Their forest homes were being destroyed to make way for villages. That meant there was

less food for the chimps to eat and less land for them to roam in. There had been about a million chimps in Africa when Jane first arrived. Thirty years later, that number was down to about three hundred thousand.

Jane began a program called TACARE (Take Care). Through it, more than a million trees have been planted in Africa to bring stripped forests back to life. TACARE also helps people living near chimp groups improve their lives.

Another of Jane's projects, ChimpanZoo, was
started to improve the lives of chimps in zoos.
Jane saw that they needed larger spaces and homes
that were more like chimp homes in the wild. She
toured labs that worked with chimps and spoke
out against labs that mistreated animals.

Today Jane still has a house in Tanzania. Grub and his children live right next door. But Jane comes to Gombe only twice a year for short visits. She spends three hundred days a year traveling around the world, giving talks to make people aware of the causes that are most important to her.

Jane's mother, Vanne, who died in 2000, always encouraged her daughter to follow her dreams. So it seems entirely fitting that Jane would want to do the same for children today. In 1991, a group of sixteen local African teenagers met with Jane and started the first Roots & Shoots club. Roots & Shoots clubs are for kids who, like young Jane, want to learn about animals as well as ways of protecting them. Now there are Roots & Shoots clubs in more 120 countries.

And to think it all started with a funny toy chimpanzee named Jubilee!

WHERE DO CHIMPS SLEEP?

CHIMPS MAKE NESTS TO SLEEP IN.
A CHIMP FINDS A PLACE
IN A TREE WHERE SEVERAL
LIMBS BRANCH OFF. IN
JUST A COUPLE OF
MINUTES, THE CHIMP
BUILDS A NEST BY
BENDING BRANCHES
TOGETHER. THIS NEST
IS WHERE THE CHIMP
WILL SLEEP THAT
NIGHT. USUALLY
A NEST IS
USED ONLY
ONCE. THE NEXT
DAY THE CHIMP
WILL BUILD A
NEW NEST IN
A NEW TREE.

TIMELINE OF
JANE GOODALL'S LIFE

1934	Born on April 3 in London, England
1938	Sister, Judy, is born on Jane's fourth birthday
1940	The Goodall family moves to Bournemouth, a seaside town in England
1952	Graduates from high school
1957	Heads to Africa for the first time on March 13
1960	Moves to the Gombe Stream Game Reserve
1964	Marries Hugo van Lawick
1967	Jane and Hugo have a son, affectionately called Grub
1971	*In the Shadow of Man,* a book about her time in Africa, is published
1974	Divorces Hugo
1975	Marries Derek Bryceson, a member of the Tanzania government
1980	Derek Bryceson dies of cancer
1986	Learns of wild chimps' threatened extinction
1991	Roots & Shoots begins with sixteen African teenagers
1994	Begins the program TACARE (Take Care)
2000	*Reason for Hope: A Spiritual Journey* is published
2002	Hugo, Jane's first husband, dies of cancer

TIMELINE OF
THE WORLD

Jubilee, a baby chimpanzee, is born at the London Zoo	1935
The first *Superman* comic book is published	1938
World War II begins in Europe	1939
The Nazis take control of France	1940
World War II ends with victory for the Allies The movie *Tarzan and the Amazons* is released	1945
Jackie Robinson becomes the first African American to play major league baseball	1947
Elvis Presley has his first number one hit record with "Heartbreak Hotel"	1957
Two states in Africa, Tanganyika and Zanzibar, form the United Republic of Tanzania	1964
A chimp named Washoe learns American Sign Language	1966
South Africa ends apartheid, an extreme form of separation of blacks and whites	1993
Nelson Mandela becomes the first black president of South Africa Stevie Nicks's album *Street Angel* includes "Jane," a song about Jane and her work	1994
An episode of *The Simpsons* features a character loosely based on Jane	2001
Barack Obama is elected president of the United States	2008

BIBLIOGRAPHY

*Bardhan-Quallen, Sudipta. **Up Close: Jane Goodall.** New York: Viking, 2008.

Goodall, Jane, and Phillip Berman. **Reason for Hope: A Spiritual Journey.** New York: Grand Central, 1999.

Goodall, Jane, with the Jane Goodall Institute. **Jane Goodall: 50 Years at Gombe.** New York: Stewart, Tabori & Chang, 2010.

Goodall, Jane. **In the Shadow of Man,** rev. ed. New York: Mariner Books, 2000.

*McDonnell, Patrick. **Me . . . Jane.** New York: Little, Brown, 2011.

*Winter, Jeanette. **The Watcher: Jane Goodall's Life with the Chimps.** New York: Schwartz & Wade, 2011.

*Books for young readers